Divine Copywriting – A Philosopher's Guide to Profound Profits!

-Volume I: The Seeds of Conscious Copy-

Jon Low

Copyright © 2013 Jon Low

All rights reserved.

ISBN: 1494844052
ISBN-13: 9781494844059

DEDICATION

I dedicate this to my entire family (especially my father and mother), and close mentors, who provided undying support and confidence in my ability to create my own version of a successful and fulfilling life. Getting on the 'Road Less Taken' to earn a full-time living doing something you love, can be by far one of the scariest and uncertain times you can experience in life. And today, I am grateful to be able to share the simple and powerful principles that helped make the difference for me.

CONTENTS

	Acknowledgments	i
1	A Message to You	1
2	Man Who Don't Like to Sell, Is Idiot	Pg 3
3	Man Who Try to Please Everyone, End Up Pleasing No One	Pg 8
4	Man Who Sells to Himself, Will Never Make Others Buy	Pg 13
5	Man Who Correct Himself While He Write is Schizophrenic	Pg 17
6	Only Immortal Man Can Wait for Perfection	Pg 22
7	Man with Unfinished Copy Create Unfinished Business	Pg 29
8	Many Words Strung Together Are Like Artworks with Meanings	Pg 32
9	Man's Sweetest Voice is His Own	Pg 37
10	We All Same-Same But Different	Pg 40
11	References	Pg 42

ACKNOWLEDGMENTS

To my father Mr. Low Oh Cheng, whom at the time of writing this book, was courageously battling stage IV cancer at the age of 77. Dad has always been a disciplined man, with a heart and love for his children that ran deep. Dad saw a strength within me that allowed me to succeed and grow during many difficult times in life. Throughout his condition, he reassured me that I was doing the best I could, and that the greatest gift I could give him was to chase my dreams furiously and only look back to pay respects and gratitude. I thank him for my life, I respect his human experiences of both joy and suffering, and I am well on my way.

To my mother Mrs. Low (Tam) Mai Mai, who has always been one of the strongest ladies I have ever known in life. Mum is physically quite small, yet her soul and energetic shine is cosmic. She has always seen greatness in me, and has always supported me no matter what strange and risky choices I made in life. At times she felt at lost, yet even guilty, perceiving that she had not given me enough choices in life. That's bollocks of course. I thank mum for my life, I respect her success in raising me as her son, and I am well on my way.

I would like to acknowledge Jeffrey Slayter for having mentored me and shared his expertise in the space of business performance. Jeffrey saw a huge potential within me that had only been partially expressed, and decided to relate to me as the 'bigger future version'. Thankfully, I walked into that image and within a short space of time, have experienced expanded results in all areas of my life; vocation, relationships, health and spirituality. Together, we are leaving a mark that the children of our children will read in their history studies. That a handful of humanitarians stood for a change in this world, and that their messages are resonating for many years to come.

1 A MESSAGE TO YOU

Dear Friend,

So glad you downloaded the *Philosopher's Guide to Divine Copy.*

If you are *curious* about how to write great copy, then the whole "sales psychology" thing probably isn't new to you.

All that may be missing is how to use sales psychology in *written form*, ink your ninja-sales guru persona on paper, let him (or her) work for your business day and night, and watch your sales figures go up!

It's like a Passive Sales Strategy!

Sounds pretty darn good doesn't it?

Thankfully, just like this guide, the internet is *plastered* with resources on how to write sales copy that actually sells, and to name a few:

- *Scientific Advertising* by Claude Hopkins
- *The Robert Collier Letter Book* by Robert Collier (highly recommended)
- *The Gary Halbert Letter* by Gary Halbert
- *Marketing Bullets* by Gary Bencivenga
- *Hypnotic Writing* by Dr. Joe Vitale
- Anything by John Carlton and Dan Kennedy…

Tactics, tools, techniques, persuasion 101 info, traditional hypnosis, neuro-linguistic programming…you name it, it's *all available* within a matter of clicks for you.

So What?

<u>Point is</u> – If you really wanted to learn how to write effective copy, there's absolutely nothing stopping you from becoming *pretty darn good* without even having to *pay a cent*.

That's especially true in this day and age where *digital* information on just about any topic is available. Google, Amazon, iPads, Blogs, Free E-books, YouTube…there is no shortage.

Info has become *dirt cheap*. Great…

So What Are You Going to Give Me that's <u>*Different*</u> Jon?

That's a good question to ask smarty-pants! ☺

While I'd be overjoyed for you to make a killing by ransacking all the great copywriting knowledge that's available online these days, there is actually a *critical point* I want to drive home.

Read on.

You see, having spent over 5 years of full-time study and application of copywriting principles, it has *always* plagued me how many of my peers have read almost every copywriting 101 principles yet *never* put them into action to get the results they want.

What the ['unpleasant word'] is Going On???

So while my client base grew, and my income made its way to 6 figures, they were still *bumming* on their couches and in cafes eating hot chips, drinking stale coffee and reading the *next big thing* on online marketing and copywriting.

For some *strange reason*, they thought that reading inspiring and amazing "how to" information *directly* translated to getting results (or even getting things done for that matter!)…

They Confused 'Absorbing' Information with Practical Application

You've seen this happen before haven't you?

How I *wish* I could just sit on my butt with a book, and have my bank account tick over with every word I read! ☺ In fact, how I wish *both* of us could.

It's a nice thought. But truth is – we would be totally *out of reality* (yet, there is a time and place for everything).

Onward.

So what's causing this seemingly absurd behavior? Why is it that the *majority* never put amazing tacit information to play, and create those results they want for their businesses?

I mean surely we can't always blame *The Secret* (by Rhonda Byrne) for all the people with the "Sit on Your Butt and Get Rich" mindset.

Clearly something is holding them back. And as much as you and I have both probably seen, it's *unconscious* to the majority. Yet that "something" needs to change in order for anybody to be effective at copywriting.

Necessary? Yes.

Nice? Not a chance.

That unconscious hold-back I am talking about is a *mindset* thing, and takes the forms of sabotaging beliefs, fears, self-doubts, procrastination , confusion and any trashy self-talk you can think of…

It's like a Little Voice in Their Heads that Persuasively Keeps Them Stuck!

It's the same familiar voice that causes people to confuse inspiration for action, spending on new stuff instead of earning, putting stuff in the way so they never have time etc…

Of course, that ultimately leaves them in a repeating loop of frustration and disappointment year after year…

Hamsters on their Own Wheels that they Can't Even See!

And if we could only get them out of the wheels and running on the road, they could cover greater distances and get better results in a *matter of minutes!*

Better yet, if *you* can identify and tweak anything that may be holding *you* back *mentally*, your results will be amplified too!

Thankfully, now we know the problem, all we have to do is *hijack* your mindset and transform bits of it (whatever is necessary) into something that is actually going to be useful for writing effective copy.

It's easier said than done of course.

So in this cool mini-book I'm going to *blend* useful and tactical information about copywriting with an *inner game* and *performance mindset* flavor so that two things happen:

1. You learn useful, timeless copywriting techniques that are a blend of material from *modern day* and *historical copywriting greats*.
2. As you read the analogies and language patterns, you will effortlessly enhance your *mental capacity* to take all that information and *apply it immediately* to get results for your business!

It's Like Copywriting and Performance Psychology - *All In One*

I can't promise that it will tweak your entire mindset as everyone has their own unique footprint of beliefs, habits, behaviors and motives.

But – This book will give you plenty of distinctions to get you well on your way.

If Confucius, Socrates, Voltaire, Leonardo Da Vinci, Aristotle, the Dalai Lama and any other great Polymaths were *covert copywriters* for their ages, then this book is my version of what I think they would have had to say on the matter…

Welcome the Philosopher's Guide to Divine

Copywriting!

Of course – It's pretty obvious these *epic people* could have been genius copywriters! ☺

For the Love of Wisdom (*Philo-Sophia*),

Jon Low
www.jon-low.com
Copywriter, Author, Philosopher

(P.S. Aside from being able to write effective copy, as you read and absorb every bit of material in this book, you will notice an enhanced; peace of mind, relationship with self, and holographic improvement in all aspects of your life)

(P.P.S. You already have within you, the latent potential for writing great copy. Trust yourself.)

(P.P.P.S. There is a Delphic Maxim that says "Know Thyself"…I'm saying, if you "Know Thyself, You Shall Know Thy Customer, and Be Able to Sell them Stuff")

(P.P.P.P.S. Note, that in some instances, I will be using very "FOB" or "Crappy" English in an attempt to deliberately sound like an old wise eastern-man)

2 MAN WHO DON'T LIKE TO SELL, IS IDIOT

One of the most frustrating things that any person who is teaching sales, marketing or copywriting to is the *art of sales*…

Not because the art of sales is actually difficult or complex to teach. It has almost *nothing* to do with that.

The problem most people have is a fundamental *aversion* to the concept of selling…and somehow, they think that copywriting is a *less shameful* form of being a salesman.

They can hide out in their words, because the person who is doing the sell isn't them…but what they write. Which actually has its benefits, but going in with that mindset is going to be *costly* when it comes to copy which I'll explain soon.

The Biggest Obstacle is Believing that being a Sales Person is like having a Fundamental Character Flaw

That may be true for some people, because I can't argue that some sales people just make me want to puke.

But on the other side, people who want to sell and have some silly beliefs that selling is wrong, distasteful and are in denial to the essential fact that you *are a sales person* is just as *puke-worthy*.

I find it ridiculous that people would choose to be a copywriter or enter a marketing or advertising-type role and be allergic to sales themselves.

"Oh I don't like selling"
"Oh that's a bit too salesy"
"Nah I don't want to be too pushy…they might get turned off"
"Hmm…nah, I don't want to ask them for money"
"I don't want to be one of *those* people"

I even once met a copywriter (she shall not be named) who told me she doesn't like *selling her own service*…What the *#@$???

Wake up.

If not, you're simply being pretentious, tip-toey, shameful and it reminds me of the feeling I get when someone overtly tells a group of people "Oh...I try not to judge"...

Get Real – You Are In Sales Whether You Like It Or Not

If you are human (and I hope you are because Aliens freak me out) then you are already in the business of sales.

The moment you get out of bed in the morning and get dressed to go out into the world, you are selling an impression you want others to have of you.

For guys and gals, when you walk into the bar you want to attract the opposite sex (or the same – you choose) by wisely choosing what you drink. Choosing what you say.

And in some instances, going to the toilet to check on your *how you look* to make sure it's somewhat *attractive* to the opposite sex.

For biz owners, when you meet clients or other professionals, you engage in small talk and all sorts of other "dry" conversations in order to build *trust* and *rapport*.

Yeah...by nature, you are already selling and being *manipulative*, so if you think 'ill' of selling, then you might well be a *contradiction* to your own existence.

It is Within Human Nature to Sell

The important thing to focus on is *how to sell well*. So let's pull together a useful way of relating to sales.

Read on.

If you don't honor that you are in sales, you aren't going to give your customers the *push* they need to get on board.

You are going to come off as *inauthentic* and you will lack the *energetic experience* to draw attention to what you want to share!

How you feel about selling is how your copy is how your reader is going to feel

So if you are ashamed of selling, your copy is going to be like someone approaching you with their head down, shoulders slump and asking you in a soft-tone voice… "Erm..um…I uhh…got something to share with you, but um…I just don't mean to be pushy and…"

Response – "Bog off, your pitiful existence is a waste of my time!"

<u>So here's what where we are going</u> - I'm going to open your eyes to an *entirely* different view of sales as you see it.

I'd like you to consider the possibility that you aren't so much allergic to selling or the fact that sales people are non-integrous jerks.

Consider that what you are actually turned off to is being *badly sold* something that you don't want any way! Like…

- Someone trying to force sell you anti-fungal foot cream when in reality, you just have some silly *earache*.
- Someone selling you a personal development product on Facebook when all you are *really curious* about at the time, is "what are my friends up to?"
- Having some advertisement pop up to play online games when you are just trying to read an info-blog post on some *interesting topic* (say – making healthy tasty food)

If that's what it means to be a sales person then by all means, sales is definitely for butt scratching space-takers.

We Aren't So Much Averse to Sales People, as We Are to Being Badly Sold To!

The art of "sales" is none other than the art of *exchange* where you make money by solving a potential problem your customer has.

(*Note:* I only advocate the sale of products that *actually* improve peoples' lives. If that's not you please stop reading now.)

Your product or service should *change* someone's life for the better, and in exchange, you must benefit too:

1. You add *value* to your buyers' life
2. You get *money* in exchange
3. The world just became a *better place*

Sales is An Opportunity for the Seller to Improve the Buyers' Life

Put it this way – If you have something that can improve someone's' life, then you *have* a responsibility to share it and sell it to as many people as you can because an ungiven gift to someone's life is like *no gift* at all!

But to do that, you have respectfully put it to them in the best way possible so they can have the solution.

You like most people, have been either badly sold to or misdirected at some point in your life. You have your personal trust issues, objections, skepticisms and fears of what could go wrong when buying a product or service.

So to guide your buyers to the point of sale (i.e. where you can change their life!) you have to do a lot of work to get them there, for example…

- *Grab their attention* with red bolded headlines and ugly formats.
- *Establish* if what you have on offer is actually *relevant* to their lives.
- Having them really *feel their pain* (not nice, but necessary).
- Making *cheesy promises and guarantees* to create hope for their lives.
- *Talking it up* a bit to establish credibility (this may include the use of testimonials).
- Answering a lot of *objections and concerns* they may have.
- *Pressuring them to act* by using scare-tactics based on scarcity and time-limits.

And this can be a lengthy seemingly *absurd process* to go through, or to have your potential customer experience.

But remember, if it is relevant to their life…they *will* want to be sold to.

Do What It Takes So They Can Have the Positive Outcome You Know You Can Deliver!

I dare say in some instances, if your product or service could actually *change* someone's life for the better, the idea that you are *not selling* is by very nature — a *primary* sin.

3 MAN WHO TRY TO PLEASE EVERYONE, END UP PLEASING NO ONE

Have you ever had the experience of trying to please everyone in your life to *keep the peace*? I certainly have, and maybe you can relate to this…

For a long part of my life, I have always tried to be a *rescuer* by saving everyone I could.

Because of some early childhood disappointment I experienced (relating to mum and dad), I spent a good part of my life trying to *please* people so that I would never have to experience that sort of disappointment again…things like:

- Saying what people wanted to hear rather than what they *needed* to hear.
- Mothering someone and taking them away from the reality of their situation.
- Going to a party and making sure I socialize with everyone with small talk that surmounts to a minute.

That sort of nonsense!

Paradoxically, what I find more often than not, is that when I try to please someone I always end up disappointing someone all the same. It totally backfires!

Trying to Please Everyone is Futile

Having this sort of mindset can really stuff up the copy you write, because if you try to talk to a *specific customer* and try to *please all customers* at the same time…you will find that your copy won't hold their attention, and even worse…it just won't flow.

You will end up sounding like someone on a coffee table trying to have a deep, meaningful, and personable conversation with *10 people* at the same time.

And the people trying to make sense of what you are saying will be *humorously* bearing witness to what appears to be someone with an *outrageous* form of ADHD…

It's Confusing and People Will Lose Attention

<u>So here's how we are going to do it</u> – Get focused on *one type of customer* and give your full attention to addressing them.

In marketing of course, it is about being *targeted*. If you are generic and try to address *multiple markets* at the same time, you may lose conversions. Not to say your copy won't work…but it may not be as effective!

If you go back to the coffee table example, imagine you just focus on having a conversation with *one person* at that table, deepen the connection with him/her and notice that everyone else will branch off into their own little conversations and leave you two alone.

Of course in an online marketing environment, this "one person" at the coffee table is representative to many people of the *same target audience*.

When Your Customer Has the Experience You Are Focusing on Them, They will Focus on You!

<u>Tip</u> – When writing your copy, create an imaginary person who is representative of your target audience, put them in front of you like you are having a conversation over coffee.

Then write that conversation you would have! Imagine what that type of person might say, what concerns they may have, and what they might want *clarified*.

You will be *amazed* at how natural your copy will be.

I'll share an inspiring experience I read about the legendary copywriter Robert Collier. Robert Collier sold almost everything you can think of under the sun in the 1930's, using direct mail copy.

One of his campaigns involved helping a client rid himself of designer-rain coats. The campaign wasn't doing so well despite how *unique* the product was so Robert was called to the rescue! I mean, designer raincoats? Come one…who wouldn't want that right?

So here's what Robert did…he sold the same rain coats to *different* markets by writing copy to them that made them feel like those *designer raincoats* were specifically made for them! Undertakers and doctors for example…

<u>For undertakers</u> - he would identify with their situation by telling them how annoying it was to have to host an outdoor funeral in the rain and have their suits damaged by the water.

He told them how their designer raincoats looked professional enough for them to wear at a funeral respectfully, whilst providing protection to their expensive suits.

<u>For doctors</u> - he identified with their frustrations of having to carry out emergencies in wet weather, without having a raincoat that looked respectful, and had the utility to hold medical supplies.

He focused on pockets the coat had, and the comfort it provided for doctors on the go.

I leave you to guess how well he sold ☺

Make Your Customer Feel Super Special and Privileged!

So let me give you an example of how I might use this principle. Suppose I wanted to sell and market this book you are reading.

One audience I might sell to <u>*aspiring copywriters*</u> who feel like they have bought *every book* on copywriting on the planet, yet *still feel* stuck when it comes to putting fingers to their keyboards.

They might experience the frustration of knowing so much and applying so little, and month after month telling themselves "I have to do this…" or "I should have done this by now…" or "I need to get more customers but…

I might also sell it to the <u>*successful small business consultants*</u> who really understands their target clients, delivers value to them, and wants a *simple guide* to DIY copywriting so they don't have to be the "best kept secret" in their industry anymore.

Another crowd that comes to mind are *business owners* and *entrepreneurs* who want to understand the essential principles of copywriting, so they can identify the right copywriter to outsource it to, and personally *validate* the quality of their work.

These people don't have much time to read an extensive book about copywriting, but they do have enough time to keep a mini-book about it so they can ask the right questions, poke holes in their own copywriter's work, and keep tabs on the quality of their overall marketing campaigns.

So Remember – Talk to One Type of Person, and Really Get Into Their World

4 MAN WHO SELLS TO HIMSELF, WILL NEVER MAKE OTHERS BUY

This is a lead on from Chapter 2 and is about deepening the understanding of getting into someone else's shoes.

I know you may have heard this before because everyone talks about it, it has just become sooo *clichéd*. But it's important.

The difference here is I am actually going to guide you through a simple exercise to really experience this principle.

I'm going to deliver you a *step by step* approach to getting into someone else's shoes rather than simply telling you to do it.

Onward.

The first step is to *meet them where they are* rather than places they *might have been*. Unless you do, it'd be as inconvenient as offering a handshake to someone who is carrying three loads of boxes.

Strange I know, but that's exactly what most people do when they try to "get into their customers' shoes". Let me give you an example…

Imagine that some dude owns a fruit store in the middle of the city and as a gentleman walks past him on the way to work, he harasses him and says "Have an apple because I reckon they taste great and if you buy 1, you will get 1 free!"

Translated to mean – "I sell good apples, and I know that, so you should too, and therefore you should buy one…and I'm even so generous that I'll give you 2!"

Whilst a little voice in the gentleman's head provides the knee-jerk response…

"Like I Give a Stuff!"

It might be the middle of winter and all this gentleman wants is a heart-warming drink to keep his fingers and chest warm from the biting 'cold as ice' blizzard. There he walks, occupied by the cold as he makes his way to his *miserable* office job in the city.

Here's a thought - Maybe if Mr. Fruit man chopped up some fruit and sold some "Gluwein" (Warmed red wine mixed with chopped up fruit) and told the gentleman…

"Why not warm yourself up with a glowing hot mug of red wine with *real* fruit? It will help you relax and temporarily relieve you of the stresses that come with the daily grind…"

The guy might even buy a few mugs of it, hang out there, and get stupid-drunk and call-in sick!

Yes – it might take an adjustment to your product, but besides, why would you try selling something that no one wants?

You Are Rarely Ever Your Own Customer, So Why Sell It to Yourself?

I find this whole game of getting outside your own ego and into that of your customers, one of the most fascinating parts of sales.

Why? It takes personal development and maturity to do it. It takes compassion, care and an utmost genuine interest in someone else's life.

And that's something you can't *teach*, it is learnt through *living* life and being *humbled* by its experiences.

But Alas! There is a way to *fast-track* this process.

So Jon, how do I Get Rid of this "Me Me-itis" Syndrome that's Costing me Money??

You don't…you will never get rid of it as long as you live because it gives you an identity, which is necessary if you want to "exist" in this world.

But what we can do is temporary *shift* that identity, to the other persons.

Here's how…remember that in Chapter 1, it is about focusing on delivering *value* to your customer less so making the sale. Therefore you have to collapse two things.

1. What Success Means for You
2. What Success Means for Your Customer

Sit there and imagine then, that your prospects happiness is your happiness…and that you will do anything to make sure they get what they want!

Just imagine you are having a conversation across a dining table, and that someone has come to you for console, expressing their tough life problems in hope that you can solve it…

…What sorts of questions might you be asking them? What are you curious to discover more about?…

(Write it down)

…What do you think might be important to them in life right now?…

(Write it down)

…what other problems might they be experiencing in life?…

…what have they tried before that hasn't worked out for them?…

(Write it down)

…what could their life look like if your solution could fulfil their needs?…

…what might you want to say to them to put them at ease?…

(Write it down)

And as you sit there experiencing what your customer is experiencing, notice that both of you are striving for a better life….one where you sell more of your products to make a living, and one where he or she is looking for a better life too.

You Both In Essence, Want the Same Thing

Notice the weight that life puts on everyone's shoulders, and that everything on the surface is by *far* what it seems. Or as mountaineer *Wanda Rutkiewicz* says…

"Everyone has their own Everest to climb"

Respect comes to mind when you get this.

So maybe your copy would improve if you spent more of your day observing human behavior, interacting with others and deeply try to get a sense of what is going on in their worlds.

At first, you will have to *hallucinate* a little to imagine what they are going through. But trust it. Whilst we all have *unique* lives, in essence, we are all the same. The insights you get will be priceless.

When you spend time to imagine what everyone else's Everest is like, the copy you write for them will almost make you cry.

Give Yourself Permission to Imagine What Their World is Like

<u>Truth</u> – sometimes when I shift into another person's shoes, I experience their sadness, frustration and grief in life. And when I imagine the thoughts they are having, the pressures of a busy life, raising kids and the exhaustion of doing something they don't love… it hurts damn it!

To top it off, people are so distrustful these days because of all the false promises and unmet promises they have experienced in their lives.

From being bullied as children, pressured by social circles or mislead by marketing scams…they have had enough!

For most, their problem is something that they probably don't believe there is a solution for.

They are taking a risk even talking to you yet alone giving you their hard-earned money. And even then, they aren't confident it will deliver those results…

Your Prospects Are Like Timid Innocent Children Who Don't Want to Be Hurt Again – Ever!

The odds are truly against you when you sell. Understand, appreciate it, and hold your customers' hands *every step* of the way if you want to tip them in your favour.

All they want is a lil' TLC ☺

> *"The best way to resolve any problem in the human world is for all sides to sit down and talk"* – **Dalai Lama**

5 MAN WHO CORRECT HIMSELF WHILE HE WRITE IS SCHIZOPHRENIC

Ever get to your computer to write and then suddenly experience *writer's block*? Like you don't know where to start?

Or worse yet, get started writing something, and repeatedly back track to change the last five words you have written?

I sure have, in fact…I just did it right now. ☺

Sometimes I have to remind myself that rather than self-editing my writing or second-guessing what it is I want to say…I should just let things flow naturally.

Because hesitating whilst writing can be as crazy as hearing someone talk to himself whilst talking to you.

It's Like Bearing Witness to a Schizophrenic Dialogue!

And of course, like the theme I so often mention, if you experience hesitation when you write the words…well, your reader is going to experience that hesitation too.

And guess what? If they experience hesitation, do you think they are likely to buy from you?

Nope.

Now I'm not saying that you shouldn't edit your copy. Far from it.

What I'm saying is that you ought to get as much of your message down on paper as possible without editing, then go back and cut, chop and change the words.

One of my favorite quotes that come to mind is from Michelangelo regarding how he carved the Statue of David…

"It is easy. You just chip away the stone that doesn't look like David."

But first you got to get the raw material out in front of you (i.e. the block of stone). In this case it happens to be words.

So sometimes you have to remind yourself time and again, that writing copy and getting into flow is like laying out all the raw material (AKA –block of stone) you need in order to communicate your offering to your future customers.

Sometimes, if you feel like you aren't making the progress you want with my words, simply close your eyes, and imagine that your written dialogue is a record of an imaginary conversation you are having with your target customers.

If I were face to face with another person, talking to them about a potential product or service that could improve their lives or solve a problem of theirs, by no means would I be self-editing my talk whilst trying to explain to them.

I might clarify certain points by *wording* things in a different way to reinforce the message.

But I'm not going say for example…

"Hi, how are…I mean…wait…you well today? I mean are you well? Great I just wanted to…wait I mean…would you like…no…is earning more money for your business something you would be…wait…not would be…I mean selling more products be of interest to you? And your business?"

When what I actually mean is… "Hi, how are you? Curious – Would you be interested in selling more products to build your business?"

It would be annoying and you just wouldn't do it.

<u>*So this is what's useful to practice*</u> - close your eyes, and pretend to be talking to someone and trying your *best* to communicate something on the spot. Whatever feels right, just go with it…then edit later.

It'll save you time, it'll build your ability to think quickly on your feet, and over time…you will get so good at synchronizing your thought patterns with your fingers, that the copy will write itself simply with *a thought*.

Sometimes of course, your writing might look like gibberish and excessive blabber but remember…

Unedited Words that Flow is Your Working Material

Just get what's in you out on paper first then you can create a *refined* version of your copy.

Or as Michelangelo would say, you can chip away all the words that *aren't* part of your message to reveal your *true work of art*.

Forget about being perfect first off the bat because that's an illusion.

You might have some lucky streaks where you get it right first time, sometimes, but you have to first practice your skill to write without simultaneously self-editing…

…after all, you can't get good *and* look good at the same time ☺

So *trust yourself* and give it a go because clarity will come with *motion*, or as some famous dude once said…

"Better to be a Fool on Fire than a Genius on Ice"

6 ONLY IMMORTAL MAN CAN WAIT FOR PERFECTION

Before becoming a full-time copywriter, I used to hang out with a lot of young professionals who were working in the 9-5.

Like me, at the time, we all had "passions" we wanted to explore to earn a full-time living without *ever* having to catch public transport again.

So every year, we would *declare* our New Year's Resolutions, set some plans in place and take massive action.

But year after year, whilst I grew and played a bigger and bigger game, I noticed that they were still *declaring* the same'ol New Year's Resolution…

Curious, I asked "So how come you're saying the same thing this year as last, what happened?"

Answer – "Well, I started putting together my website together and I wanted to sell my idea, but it wasn't quite right so I couldn't sell it"…

…or "I wasn't quite ready yet…so I didn't start"… "the product is ready, it's just that I don't think the market will buy it.."

<u>But here's the thing</u> – When I dug deeper to what was going on, I realized they had in fact, created a lot of things that were 'sell-able' like; designer t-shirts from their label, custom cakes for parties and weddings, futuristic fashion blogs, photography…you name it.

But they *never* actually got around to selling it.

They didn't feel the "timing was right" or that "their product was ready" or… "that their product was different enough"…

They confused having a "Perfectly Crafted Product" with a "Marketable Product" that will <u>earn them money</u> and <u>make customers happy</u>!

So my buddies had their gifts stashed in a closet, festering to become the world's *best kept secrets* rather than being *highly valuable* products or services for the market.

Yeah – it is costly, until you can let go and understand that…

There is Rarely a Perfect Time or Place to Sell Your Product!

If you are waiting for things to be "perfect" you had better live a *very very long time*. Now I'm not saying perfection is not worth striving for, but it's certainly not worth *holding on to* because you will lose sight of the end you have in mind.

Same thing applies with your copy. Trying to tweak your sales copy to earn money, and achieve "perfection" in your sales copy before you even launch and test it on the market is *suicide*.

Copy Will Not Earn You Anything If No One Reads It!

So how do we get through this *perfection paralysis syndrome*?

We could just tell ourselves that "it's never the perfect time" so just fly it…but sometimes there is still that feeling of resistance to just letting go.

No matter how much you acknowledge it intellectually, it can seem like a *very difficult* decision to make.

If you are, then it is likely that you have collapsed two things— <u>Well Written Copy</u> and <u>Copy that Sells</u>.

The distinction you have to get is…

"Well Written Copy" and "Copy that Sells" are two *different* things

Well written copy usually includes the following core elements:

- Addresses the right target audience.
- Has a killer headline that draws their attention.

- Has a compelling story that builds rapport and connects with your customers.
- Provides magnetic benefits and solutions to their problems.
- Takes away the risk for the buyer.
- Creates scarcity to cause people to act – *now*.
- Has embedded call to actions throughout your copy
- Words that are spelt correctly etc…

Which is all great, but if you stay in the zone of having perfectly *well written copy*, I guarantee, *every time* you look back at your copy, you will find more *edits* or adjustments to be made.

If you take this approach, you will find yourself spending so much time fiddling with your copy, you will lose sight of your *primary objective* – earning more money.

Let's look at what *copy that sells* looks like:

- It has been *tested* on an audience, and proven to generate more than enough sales to cover your costs.
- It has been rigorously *split-tested* to determine what works and what doesn't.
- This whole cycle has been *rinsed* and *repeated* to <u>maximize</u> your profits, until *no further* improvement is possible.

In more cases than not, the end goal of copy is to actually make sales. And this is obviously a combination of both well written copy, and copy that has been tested.

<u>*I'll give you an analogy*</u> – To progress your copy and business, imagine that having a well written piece of copy is like having a *left leg*, and that testing your copy with the market is like your *right leg*.

Both need to happen in *sync* in order for you to move forward; Left- Right- Left-Right-Left Right…

Well Written Copy *and* Tested Copy that Sells, go Hand in Hand

"Life is pretty simple: You do some stuff. Most fails. Some works. You do more of what works. If it works big, others quickly copy it. Then you do something else. The trick is the doing something else" - **Leonardo da Vinci**

7 MAN WITH UNFINISHED COPY CREATE UNFINISHED BUSINESS

One of the recurring and *heated* debates that occur in the copywriting world is "short-form copy" versus "long-form copy". If you aren't familiar with what this may be, let me give you an insight into an experience you might be able to relate too…

Have you ever written a report, email, or SMS message and thought "Hmm…this feels kind of too wordy"?

The *exact* same thing happens in copy. Many copywriters fear writing too much and boring the hell out of their reader, and hence damaging their sales.

They feel like their copy should be shortened because people "don't have time" or are "going to lose attention".

<u>Worse yet</u> – Many web designers, graphic designers or professional markets support the view that people will just *skim* through and not really read all the words.

That's only half-true.

Some people will skim through and just pick up the info they need, but other readers will nit-pick at every point because they need more information in order to make a *buying* decision.

Simply put – There are *right brain* orientated people, and there are *left-brain* orientated people.

You Want to Cover *Both Ends* of this Spectrum

<u>But here's the thing</u> – The very idea of *long-copy* and *short-copy* is subjective and arbitrary.

There is no formal definition for what is considered "long" or considered "short".

The *common mistake* that people make is copy that is boring, irrelevant and loses your *reader's attention* is mislabeled as long-copy.

This is downright BS of course…

…if I was selling an expensive credible program for young teenage females who just got knocked up, and identified with their tragically unforeseeable situation…then I guarantee you they will read *every single word* meticulously to get all their questions and concerns answered, whilst hanging on to the hope of a resolved future!

So what you really got to get is there *is no such thing* as long or short copy.

It is Either Your Copy Says What Is Needed to Sell, Or it Doesn't!

And unlike face to face sales…with sales copy, all the information your buyer needs in order to make a purchasing decision *has to be there* or you *greatly* reduce your chances of making a sale.

So forget the illusion about copy that is short or long. The copy you are aiming for:

- ➢ Grabs the attention of your *target customer*
- ➢ Holds their attention
- ➢ Addresses their concerns
- ➢ Establishes credibility and rapport
- ➢ Creates an irresistible offer

And even if they *don't buy* immediately, they will still think about your product or service for many days to come.

Craft a Message that Sticks!

Dan Kennedy, one of the most famous marketers and copywriters today said the following…

> *"The person who says 'I would never read all that copy' makes the mistake of thinking they are the customer. And they're not. We are never our own customers. There's a thing in copywriting I teach called 'message-to-market*

match'. It is this: when your message is matched to a target market that has a high level of interest in it, not only does responsiveness go up but readership goes up, too. The whole issue of interest goes up."

Point being is, if you get in your customers' shoes rather than selling it to yourself, do not fear how long your copy will be; just make sure you tell them everything they need to know.

You would agree that people aren't exactly 100% willing to just *giving away* their money to sales people who approach them with a potential solution to their problems.

<u>Remember</u> - everyone has their concerns, objections, skepticisms and opinions which need to be resolved in order for them to buy.

For some people, that's not much and they will skim the copy to find what they need to know and buy. For others, they have a lot, meaning they will keep reading and reading until their questions are answered.

So how does this principle hold against real-data and statistics? Historically, 'longer' (not long form☺) copy outsells shorter copy consistently (confirmed by MarketingExperiments.com)!

So make sure your copy is as complete as possible…because "Unfinished Copy is Unfinished Business".

8 MANY WORDS STRUNG TOGETHER ARE LIKE ARTWORKS WITH MEANINGS

In this lovely digital age where images, videos, words and audio can be quickly and cheaply (most cases free) fused together online, it is tempting to add these other digital media to your copy to make it look appealing.

Now this isn't such a bad idea for building credibility and creating an exclusive impression. But if the pictures *get in the way* of the user's ability to read your copy with ease then you got a problem.

Consider how *outrageous* it would be if I was communicating the benefits of learning copywriting in order to sell an e-product, and next to the benefits I showed you a pretty picture of a parrot.

???

The other pressing issue of having an image in the copy is it can disrupt the flow of the message you are trying to get across. I liken it to having a conversation with a stranger over coffee.

Let me explain…

Suppose you are having a conversation with a stranger over coffee. As you warm up to each other, you might start sharing more and more *intimate* information with each other…

…then as time passes, you get drawn into what is called the "flow of conversation". This flow of conversation is beautiful state where both of you lose a sense of time, your attention is fully on one another, and anything else is considered a *side-track* for what's most important to you…

Being Deeply Engaged in the Conversation

Suppose now, that a waitress asks "Gentlemen, would you like to order anything else?" You would be quick to answer so that you can return to the conversation!

Notice that during the conversation, anything like looking at your phone, shuffling through your bag or losing eye contact is a *temporary* disruption to the flow of information exchange occurs.

Key words – <u>Disrupts the Flow</u>

In copy, the same thing occurs. Once you have your reader's attention, there is a flow that is happening between the words they are reading on the page, and their emotional experience of it.

So if you are going to use graphics, make sure they *directly support* or *reinforce* your message that you are trying to get across, rather than simply to make things look pretty.

If it disrupts the flow, or if your reader has to "look for the next word to read" on the page…then your reader could easily have their attention *hijacked* by something else (hopefully, not your competitor)!

The Flow of Your Copy is Critical

We do this all time, think about it.

If you are say doing work on your computer and an email alert pops up where does your attention immediately go?

And, if what you are doing doesn't have your *full attention*, it's very possible you will go off and read that email and before you know it…you could be fluffing about on Facebook! ☺

Assume Your Prospects Have Attention Deficit Disorder

Your job is to do everything you can to keep them in a state of attention surplus.

<u>Remember</u> - If you're going to use graphics, videos or audios, make sure they directly support your message and they aren't just there purely to make things look pretty.

But having something *visually pleasing* is still important, because professional-looking sites really help establish credibility straight off the bat. It's just about establishing the right balance.

Onward.

Once upon a time…using images in ad or sales copy, used to add *significant* costs to the print and distribution of the ad. And of course, if the cost per sale increases, the likelihood of the campaign being profitable, greatly decreases.

People Used to be Very Careful with Using Graphics in Ad Copy

A part of me believes this *limit* on ad copy back then, really helped push the greats like Robert Collier and Claude Hopkins to the heights.

It forced them to stick to the *bare basics* of written salesmanship.

So now, I'm going to give you a few tips and distinctions you can use to *maximize* aesthetics using words and formats *before* having to rely on any graphics etc…

Remember, these words you are reading right now, in their own unique fonts, are simply pictures and symbols that have been assembled to have *meaning*.

Words are just *graphics* that society has assigned meaning to!

Really try to internalize this because most people have it in their minds that *words* and *pictures* are two entirely different species…when in fact they are not.

That distinction really changed the way I wrote copy, because I realized that I was actually *painting with words*.

Your Keyboard and Pen is Your Brush!

You can use *formatting* or bullets to give your copy some visual aesthetic. Some examples include:

- Listing all the **benefits** your customers have to gain from using your product or service.
- Summarizing the key pain points that your customers are experiencing, and that you resolve.
- Providing a list of *all the potential uses* your product or service has.
- Summarizing the **key principles** or takeaways that you want to drive home before your reader leaves.

Literally anything that makes it *much easier* for your reader to absorb your piece of information, and to hold their attention.

In some cases, like emails,
You can even shorten
the margins so that your
copy is easily digestible
like packets of bite-size
information, rather than
long paragraphs of wide
copy.

Again with the tightened margins example, it is also useful to give your breathers more visual *white space*, so they can more easily process the information without having to read long and fat paragraphs of writing.

The solution would be to break up your writing into short paragraphs, just like how this book is written.

And sometimes, just *sometimes*, using word-formatting can be useful because it gives your writing a particular 'tone of voice' that makes the reader-experience simple, and also helps you to *drive home* a particularly important point.

I think you get my point.

There are a number of other ways that you can also employ in order to "sex-up" the visual appeal of your writing to support your message.

Sometimes, if you want to drive home a profound statement, you can choose to center-bold it to stand out in your writing...

There Are No Limits to What You Can Do With Your Writing – You Choose!

9 MAN'S SWEETEST VOICE IS HIS OWN

There are many takes on what is happening here. As you read every word that is written on this page, notice that the only way you are interpreting it is well…by actually reading it yourself in your own voice.

Now that doesn't mean you are reading it out loud. It means there is a voice in your head (your voice) that is reading these words and speaking directly to you. It's trippy isn't it?

But this is an *important distinction* to get…

Your Readers Aren't Reading Your Copy, They are Talking to Themselves!

Just like you are doing now as you read every word on this page.

Robert Collier once pointed out an important principle at play when writing copy… "Always enter the conversation already occurring in the customer's mind".

Great advice Robby! Because when we absorb that element with the fact that your readers are actually talking to themselves rather than simply reading your copy, then you now have the formulae for making sure your sales message sticks.

1. You get on their "thought bus".
2. You influence and guide their thought bus.
3. You make the sale.

Deep, but bear with me because it's a *huge* opportunity to do a lot of things.

For one, the longer you hold your reader's attention, the more familiar and comfortable they will get with what you have to share. This explains why the level of readership tends to stay the same after the first couple of hundred words.

Basically, within the first few hundred words, the people who find what you have to share *irrelevant* to the conversation that's happening in their head, will not read any further. Beyond that, people will normally read more of what you have to say.

So the question to *always* ask yourself…

"What is Going on in My Customers' Minds at the Point they are Reading This?"

For some people, it's "I got to put the kids to sleep", or for others it is "How am I going to pay the bills?" In the case of teenage males and females, it might be "What's Everyone Else Doing to Hang Out?"

Whatever is going on in their head is your *entry point* for copy, from which you can use to maneuver them towards what you are trying to sell.

If you were writing copy to sell your *au pair* services, then these are some sample entry points you could use in a subject line or heading:

"I Got to Put the Kids to Sleep!" – That's What Most Busy Mothers Told Me Before They Discovered What I Could Do…

"How Am I Going to Pay The Bills?" – Hard Working Fathers Couldn't Find an Answer To this Question…till they Spent 5 minutes With Me!

"What's Everyone Else Doing to Hang Out??" – The Burning Question that Most Teenagers who Care for Their Baby Siblings Want to Know…

But there's more to this *internal dialogue* thing that meets the eye. The longer your copy helps them hold that conversation in their head, the more *rapport* you build, which leaves them open to suggestion and commands.

Things like "buy this now" and "get excited or "take action now". These are commands they would normally have an *allergic reaction* to until you have established a high level of trust!

Never Introduce a Hard-Sell Before Reaching the Highest Point of Rapport

When writing copy, it is this *very reason* that we normally don't make blatantly obvious buying requests until *much later* in the written piece.

10 WE ALL SAME-SAME BUT DIFFERENT

As a finishing remark, realize that writing effective copy takes a lot of inner game. Realize that everyone, you and I, are pretty much the *same* on a fundamental level. We simply *express* ourselves in different shapes and forms.

So as humans, we all have our concerns, our fears, our internal conversations and knee-jerk reactions to events that surround our lives. And even more so when it comes to people trying to *sell us* stuff! ☺

But this is a *great opportunity* because at some level, if you understand and acknowledge the very things that make you human, you will also understand a lot about what others are going through in their lives too.

You Already Have the *Insider's Scoop* for What's Going on In Peoples' Lives!

The better you can relate to yourself, the better you will be able to relate to others too.

Beyond simply learning the techniques and tools to write effective copy, much of it relies on your *life experience* and your ability to make sense of the world and other people.

Take the time to reflect and deepen your relationship with yourself, and get curious about what drives other people too. Because as you go through discover what it means to be *human* notice that others are taking that journey too…

You will realize we all want very similar things.

So to effectively lead people on different journeys, it is then helpful to have been on the block for a bit and walked down some tracks that most others would consider *new ground*.

Be an Explorer First, then You Can Become the Guide

I wish you well,

Jon Low
www.jon-low.com
Copywriter, Author, Philosopher

11 REFERENCES

- *Scientific Advertising* by Claude Hopkins
- *The Robert Collier Letter Book* by Robert Collier
- *The Ultimate Sales Letter* by Dan Kennedy
- *The Gary Halbert Letter* by Gary Halbert (www.thegaryhalbertletter.com)
- *Marketing Bullets* by Gary Bencivenga (www.marketingbullets.com)
- *Hypnotic Writing* by Dr. Joe Vitale

ABOUT THE AUTHOR

Jon Low is a Copywriter, Author, and Philosopher with over 10 years of experience in the spaces of human potential, practical psychology, business performance and eastern philosophies. He has worked with hundreds of people across multinational corporates and all walks of life including; global entrepreneurs, sports personalities, CEOs, young professionals, coaches *and* consultants. In carrying out his services, Jon has been able to help his clients *identify* the *smallest of shifts* that make the biggest differences for their lives and businesses – *today*.

Jon's mission is to help others get clear on their version of a joyous and fulfilling life, and to provide them with the necessary resources to fully express their gifts to the world.

www.jon-low.com

www.ingramcontent.com/pod-product-compliance
Lightning Source LLC
Chambersburg PA
CBHW051822170526
45167CB00005B/2121